Research Comparing the Emotional Intelligence

of Criminal Justice College Students in

Experiential and Didactic Programs

Wayne L. Davis, Ph.D.

Paul J. Leslie, Ed.D.

Rev. date: 11/04/2016

To order additional copies of this book, contact:
Xlibris
1-888-795-4274
www.Xlibris.com
Orders@Xlibris.com
738561

Research Comparing the Emotional Intelligence of Criminal Justice College Students in Experiential and Didactic Programs

Wayne L. Davis, Ph.D.

Lincoln Memorial University

Harrogate, TN

Paul J. Leslie, Ed.D.

Aiken Technical College

Aiken, SC

Illustrators

Ariana Greer

Derrick Freeman

Brandon Lutterman

Authors

Wayne L. Davis, Ph.D.

Wayne L. Davis holds a Bachelor of Science in Electrical Engineering from the University of Michigan-Dearborn, a Master of Science in Business Administration from Madonna University, and a Ph.D. in Criminal Justice from Capella University. Dr. Davis has graduated from city, state, and federal law enforcement academies and he has over 20 years of law enforcement experience with city, state, and federal law enforcement agencies. Dr. Davis was a field training officer with the Indiana State Police and has received the U.S. Customs & Border Protection Commissioner's Award.

Dr. Davis recently served as a visiting professor at Liaocheng University in China. Dr. Davis currently teaches graduate level research courses and serves on thesis and dissertation committees at Lincoln Memorial University in Harrogate, TN.

Wayne L. Davis, Ph.D.

Paul J. Leslie, Ed.D.

Paul J. Leslie holds a Bachelor of Arts in History from Armstrong Atlantic University in Savannah, Georgia and a Doctorate in Counseling Psychology from Argosy University in Sarasota, Florida. Currently, he serves as Academic Coordinator of Psychology at Aiken Technical College where he is also an advisor in the Human Services degree program and teaches courses in abnormal psychopathology, substance abuse counseling, and interviewing techniques. Dr. Leslie is a Licensed Counselor and a Human Services - Board Certified Practitioner. He has a private practice in counseling, coaching and clinical hypnotherapy in Aiken, South Carolina.

Paul J. Leslie, Ed.D.

Table of Contents

Preface

This is the fourth academic research study that the authors have conducted on the emotional intelligence of college students. All four studies involved using the 33 item Schutte, Malouff, Hall, Haggerty, Cooper, Golden and Dornheim (1998) Emotional Intelligence Scale to measure levels of emotional intelligence. Study 1 compared criminal justice students who were enrolled in an experiential program to other students at the same two-year technical college. Study 2 compared nursing and human services students who were enrolled in an experiential program to general education students who were enrolled in a didactic program at the same two-year technical college. Study 3 compared criminal justice and psychology students who were enrolled in didactic programs to other students who were enrolled in experiential programs at the same four-year college. The current study compares the emotional intelligence of criminal justice students who were enrolled in an experiential program at a two-year technical college to the emotional intelligence of criminal justice students who were enrolled in a didactic program at a four-year liberal arts college.

CHAPTER 1

Summary of First Three Studies on

Emotional Intelligence

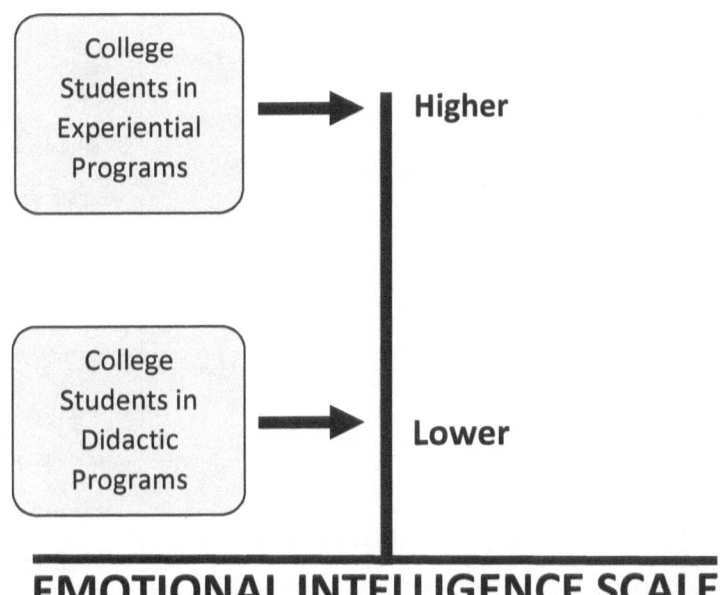

SUMMARY OF STUDY 1 (Davis & Leslie, 2014)

Study #	Focus of Study 1	Significant Results	Explanation
1	The emotional intelligence of criminal justice students who were enrolled in an experiential program with extensive hands-on exercises were compared to other students at the same two-year technical college. **Participants:** Extensive Hands-on Training • Criminal Justice Students • Nursing Students Moderate Hands-on Training • Human Services Students Nominal Hands-on Training • General Education Students	There was a significant difference between the students in the criminal justice and general education programs. Although the criminal justice students displayed a higher emotional intelligence than did the nursing and human services students, there was no significant difference between the scores. Ethnicity, age, and sex had no impact on emotional intelligence.	The more hands-on training, the higher the emotional intelligence. The criminal justice students at the college had more classes that specifically trained the students for some of the factors measured on the emotional intelligence instrument, which clearly distinguished them from the general education students.

Figure 1. Criminal justice students in the experiential program practicing interrogation techniques.

Figure 2. Criminal justice students in the experiential program practicing interviewing techniques.

Figure 3. Criminal justice students in the experiential program practicing defensive tactics techniques.

Summary of Study 1

The extensive hands-on training for the crimimal justice students who were enrolled in the experiential program involved practicing interrogation techniques (e.g., reading non-verbal messages and listening to a suspect's tone of voice), practicing defensive tactics (e.g., controlling own emotions and reading body language), performing the job objectively (e.g., using truth values to assess the legality of actions based on the elements of the law), making a good impressions to others (e.g., writing professional police reports), and investigating problems methodology (e.g., overcoming barriers and contradicting information). Because the criminal justice students practiced many different types of hands-on exercises, and because some of these skills were specifically assessed on the 33 item Emotional Intelligence Scale, it is not surprising that the criminal justice students scored higher in emotional intelligence than did the other students. Although the nursing students and human services students also engaged in hands-on training, they were not the same type of skills that the criminal justice students practiced.

SUMMARY OF STUDY 2 (Leslie & Davis, 2015)

Study #	Focus of Study 2	Significant Results	Explanation
2	The emotional intelligence of nursing and human services students, who were enrolled in experiential programs with hands-on exercises, were compared to general education students at the same two-year technical college. **Participants:** Extensive Hands-on Training • Nursing Students Moderate Hands-on Training • Human Services Students Nominal Hands-on Training • General Education Students	There was no significant difference between the emotional intelligence levels of students in the nursing, human services, and general education programs. Ethnicity, age, and sex were not related to emotional intelligence.	Although students in the nursing and human services programs had more hands-on training and displayed a higher emotional intelligence than did the general education students, the scores were not significantly different. The survey itself, and the questions that were asked, may not have focused on the specific emotional intelligence skills acquired by the nursing and human services students.

Figure 4. Nursing students in the experiential program

practicing CPR techniques.

Summary of Study 2

The nursing and human services students in the experiential programs practiced hands-on training that involved communicating verbally, performing the job objectively, performing the job professionally, and investigating problems methodology (e.g., overcoming barriers and contradicting information). This training did increase their level of emotional intelligence when compared to the general education students, who were enrolled in a didactic program. However, the survey itself, and the questions that were asked, may not have focused on the specific emotional intelligence skills acquired by the nursing and human services students. In other words, other surveys may better distinguish the emotional intelligence levels of nursing and human services students.

SUMMARY OF STUDY 3 (Davis & Leslie, 2015)

Study #	Focus of Study 3	Significant Results	Explanation
3	The emotional intelligence of criminal justice and psychology students who were enrolled in didactic programs were compared to other students who were enrolled in experiential programs at the same four-year college. Experiential Programs Theater Communication Arts Education Didactic Programs Criminal Justice Psychology	Students who were enrolled in the experiential programs displayed a higher level of emotional intelligence than did students who were enrolled in the didactic programs. Ethnicity, age, and sex were not related to emotional intelligence.	At the four-year liberal arts college, the criminal justice students did not engage in hands-on training. As a result, they displayed a lower level of emotional intelligence than did non-criminal justice students who did engage in hands-on training.

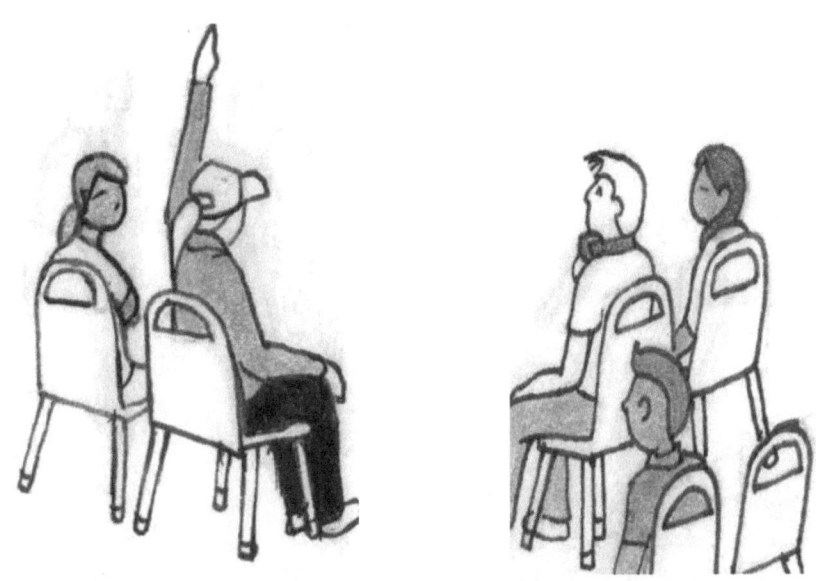

Figure 5. Criminal justice students in the didactic program

listening to a lecture in class.

Summary of Study 3

Emotional intelligence is not necessarily program dependent per se; the evidence has shown that emotional intelligence is directly related to specific hands-on training. Didactic programs involve listening to lectures, taking notes, and engaging in little, if any, hands-on exercises. The criminal justice students who were enrolled in the didactic program displayed a lower level of emotional intelligence than did students who were enrolled in non-criminal justice experential programs. In other words, students in the theator, communication arts, and education programs, who actively practiced communicating professionally, reading body language, and controlling their emotions (i.e., experiential learning), displayed a significantly higher level of emotional intelligence than did criminal justice students who were enrolled in a didactic program.

References

Davis, W.L., & Leslie, P.J. (2014). The effect of application-based training on the emotional intelligence of criminal justice students (2014). *Journal of Higher Education Theory and Practice, 14*(2), 115-121.

Davis, W.L. & Leslie, P.J. (2015). A comparison of emotional intelligence levels between students in experiential and didactic college programs (2015). *The International Journal of Emotional Education, 7*(2), 63-65.

Leslie, P.J. & Davis, W.L. (2015). Emotional Intelligence of Undergraduate Human Services Students (2015). *Journal of Human Services, 35*(1), 5-13.

CHAPTER 2

Current Study on Emotional Intelligence

Research Comparing the Emotional Intelligence of Criminal Justice College Students Who Were Enrolled in an Experiential Program to the Emotional Intelligence of Criminal Justice College Students Who Were Enrolled in a Didactic Program

Abstract

This study assessed whether there was a significant difference in the levels of emotional intelligence (EI) between criminal justice college students who were enrolled in an experiential program and criminal justice college students who were enrolled in a didactic program. The participants were given the 33 item Schutte, Malouff, Hall, Haggerty, Cooper, Golden and Dornheim (1998) Emotional Intelligence Scale to measure levels of EI. The findings indicate that there was a significant difference between the two types of programs of study with students in the application-based program exhibiting a higher level of EI. Future research may include assessing the relationship between the training of EI in criminal justice coursework and future job performance.

Introduction

There can be multiple challenges and occupational specific stressors in the field of law enforcement (Ellison, 2004; Deschamps, Paganon-Badinier, Marchand & Merele, 2003; Greene & del Carmen, 2002; He, Zhao, & Archbold, 2002). The involvement of law enforcement personnel in situations of extreme danger and stress and the changes in the economic and technological landscape have increased the work related demands imposed upon these professionals (Deschamps, et. al., 2003). In order to consistently perform effectively in the field, law enforcement personnel must have a skill set that not only includes tactical interventions but also incorporates the ability to successfully handle confrontation, display good judgment and create healthy relationships (Prazno & Prazno, 1999; Turner, 2006). Because working in the field of law enforcement is linked to emotionally charged situations, it is logical to assert that the awareness and controlling of one's own emotional state is essential to success in the field. A person's ability to successfully discern and work with emotions has been labeled

emotional intelligence (Goleman, 1995).

Interest in the impact that emotional intelligence (EI) can have on a

person's mental and emotional well-being has increased in recent years

(Goleman, 1998). Salovey and Mayer (1989) have defined EI as the

ability to perceive the emotions of oneself and others and to use this

perception in directing one's own thinking and behavior. Zeidner,

Matthews, and Roberts (2004) found that the perceiving and processing

of emotions can assist in emotional self-regulation. Mayer and Salovey

(1997) have asserted that EI also represents the ability to manage

emotions in a way that fosters personal growth. Goleman (1995)

characterizes EI as the ability to regulate one's emotions in the areas of

self-awareness, self-motivation, empathy and social skills (Goleman,

1995).

The relevance of cultivating EI in law enforcement work cannot be overstated. It has been found that in comparison to other helping professions, law enforcement personnel were generally more aware of the emotions of themselves and others, which enables them to cope more effectively with the pressures of their work (Bar-On, Brown, Kirkcaldy and Thome', 2000). In addition, Brunetto, Teo, Shacklock, and Farr-Wharton (2012) found that higher levels of EI in law enforcement personnel predicted higher rates of emotional well-being and job satisfaction. Pogrebin and Polle (1991) have asserted that the quality of work performed by law enforcement personnel has an emotional component, and success in the field entails maintaining professional conduct by being in control of one's emotions. There have also been significant correlations found between the job performance of law enforcement personnel and EI (Al Ali, Garner and Magadley, 2012).

The importance of EI has been reflected in the addition of training programs designed to increase the levels of EI in a variety of settings. Bagshaw (2000) has suggested that not only can EI be taught, but training in EI can boost an individual's level of awareness of his or her own emotions. Other studies have demonstrated an increase in the level of emotional competence in participants of EI trainings (Sardo, 2004). Slaski and Cartwright (2003) found statistically significant improvement in levels of EI after four-week training programs for project managers in EI competency. Latif (2004) found that specific training for students in EI skills (self-awareness, self-regulation, motivation, interpersonal skills and empathy) significantly increased their levels of EI when comparing scores from the beginning of the semester with those at the end of the semester. Weis and Arnesen (2007) assert that application-based training approaches to EI more often allow individuals to more effectively evaluate and judge their own behaviors than strictly analytical examinations of EI concepts.

If training in EI can lead to increased levels in a person's ability to recognize and regulate his or her own emotions while also being aware of the emotional state of others, then it makes sense to expect that this ability would be greater in those trained in law enforcement applications. Davis and Leslie (2014) found a significant difference in EI levels between application-based criminal justice college students and non-application-based general education college students. It was conjectured that the difference in EI between the two groups may have been due to the nature of the training that the criminal justice students received, which required the ability to recognize and assess emotions and body language.

The purpose of this study was to assess whether college students in an application-based criminal justice program would exhibit higher levels of emotional intelligence when compared to college students in a non-application-based criminal justice program. Because the nature of the course work in the application-based program is to teach law enforcement skills that help students to identify and control emotions (e.g., to read body language and to testify in court), it was hypothesized that students in the application-based program would exhibit higher levels of EI when compared to students in the non-application-based program. The non-application-based criminal justice program was a textbook-driven program and did not teach application-based law enforcement skills. This study additionally explored if gender, age, and ethnicity impacted EI.

Methods

Participants in this study included 89 undergraduate students who were enrolled in criminal justice programs. Forty-three students were enrolled in an application-based, two-year, technical college program. Forty-six students were enrolled in a four-year, textbook-driven, liberal arts program. Data were collected from students who were readily available and who voluntarily agreed to take the survey. The students self-identified their age (range = 18-37 years), gender (54 males, 35 females), ethnicity (52 Caucasian, 22 African-American, 9 Hispanic and 6 other), and their school (43 technical college students and 46 liberal arts students).

Participants were provided a 33 question survey to determine if there was a significant difference in the levels of EI between students in the experiential criminal justice program and students in the didactic criminal justice program. In addition to the 33 questions, demographic information was collected on age, gender, and ethnicity. Linear

regression analysis was used to assess the relationship between age and

EI, one-way analysis of variance (ANOVA) was used to assess the

difference between EI and gender and between EI and ethnicity, and an

independent-samples *t* test was used to assess the difference between EI

and type of college program.

Instrument

Participants in this study completed the Schutte, Malouff, Hall, Haggerty, Cooper, Golden and Dornheim (1998) Emotional Intelligence Scale, which consists of 33 questions (See Table 1). The scale contains three subscales: appraisal and expression of emotion in self and others (e.g., I am aware of the nonverbal messages I send to others), regulation of emotion in self and others (e.g., I have control over my emotions), and utilization of emotions in solving problems (e.g., I compliment others when they have done something well). For each item on the measure, a rating of 1 indicated "strongly disagree" and a rating of 5 indicated "strongly agree" (1988). After three responses on the survey were reverse-scored, the total score was calculated by summing the total points on the 33 items. The higher the participant's total score, the greater the individual's emotional intelligence. The instrument has shown an average score of 131 for females and 125 for males (maximum score = 33 x 5 = 165). The scale has demonstrated an internal consistency with a Cronbach's alpha of .90 and .87, a test-retest

reliability score of .78, discriminant and convergent validity when

compared to the Meyer-Salovey-Caruso Emotional Intelligence Test

(MSCEIT), and convergent validity when compared to the Trait Meta-

Mood Scale. In addition, the Emotional Intelligence Scale has shown

predictive validity by showing a significant relationship to first year

college students' grade point average (Schutte, et al., 1998).

Table 1.

The 33-item emotional intelligence scale (Schutte, et. al., 1998).

1. I know when to speak about my personal problems to others
2. When I am faced with obstacles, I remember times I faced similar obstacles and overcame them
3. I expect that I will do well on most things I try
4. Other people find it easy to confide in me
5. I find it hard to understand the non-verbal messages of other people*
6. Some of the major events in my life have led me to re-evaluate what is important and not important
7. When my mood changes, I see new possibilities
8. Emotions are one of the things that make life worth living
9. I am aware of my emotions as I experience them
10. I expect good things to happen
11. I like to share my emotions as I experience them
12. When I experience a positive emotion, I know how to make it last
13. I arrange events others enjoy
14. I seek out activities that make me happy
15. I am aware of the non-verbal messages I send to others
16. I present myself in a way that makes a good impression on others
17. When I am in a positive mood, solving problems is easy for me
18. By looking at their facial expressions, I recognize the emotions people are experiencing
19. I know why my emotions change
20. When I am in a positive mood, I am able to come up with new ideas
21. I have control over my emotions
22. I easily recognize my emotions as I experience them
23. I motivate myself by imagining a good outcome to tasks I take on
24. I compliment others when they have done something well
25. I am aware of the non-verbal signals other people send
26. When another person tells me about an important event in his or her life, I almost feel as though I have experienced this event myself
27. When I feel a change in emotions, I tend to come up with new ideas
28. When I am faced with a challenge, I give up because I believe I will fail*
29. I know what other people are feeling just by looking at them
30. I help other people feel better when they are down
31. I use good moods to help myself keep trying in the face of obstacles
32. I can tell how people are feeling by listening to the tone of their voice
33. It is difficult for me to understand why people feel the way they do*

*These items were reverse scored.

26

Results

The emotional intelligence scores were measured for all 89 students. The total sample mean was 130.72 (SD = 14.50) with a mean of 132.23 (SD = 14.96) for females and 129.74 (SD = 14.25) for males. See the table below for descriptive statistics on gender and EI. The stem and leaf plot and the Q-Q plot of emotional intelligence indicate that the distribution of the dataset is close to normal (Norusis, 2008). See Appendix for select SPSS data output.

Gender and EI (Descriptive Statistics)

Dependent Variable: Emotional Intelligence

	N	Mean	SD	SE
Females	35	132.23	14.955	2.528
Males	54	129.74	14.246	1.939
Total	89	130.72	14.498	1.537

Age and EI (Inferential Statistics)

Multiple analyses were conducted to determine what factors, if any, influence emotional intelligence. Linear regression analysis was performed on age and EI. SPSS was used to check the assumptions of linear regression. See the Appendix for select data output. The Q-Q plot of Studentized residuals indicates that the distribution of the dataset is close to normal (Norusis, 2008). The Studentized residual plot indicates that the variance of emotional intelligence is constant across age (Norusis, 2008). The Studentized residual plot makes violations of the regression assumptions easier to see and are preferred over the standardized residual plot.

A simple linear regression analysis was used to determine if the age of a student could predict EI. The results were as follows: $F(1, 87)$ = .539, p = .465. See Appendix for SPSS data output. The null hypothesis states that there is no relationship between age and EI.

The regression equation used to predict EI based on age was determined to be as follows: EI = 123.891 + .312 (age), R^2 = .006. The results of the simple linear regression analysis suggest that there is no significant relationship between student age and EI. In short, age is a poor predictor of EI.

Ethnicity and EI (Inferential Statistics)

One-way ANOVA was conducted to determine if there was a difference in emotional intelligence between different ethnicity groups. See Appendix for SPSS data output. One-way analysis of variance indicated that ethnicity did not impact EI. The results were as follows: $F(3, 85) = .092$, $p = .964$, $\alpha = .05$.

Gender and EI (Inferential Statistics)

One-way ANOVA was conducted to determine if there was a difference in emotional intelligence between males and females. See Appendix for SPSS data output. One-way ANOVA indicated that gender did not impact EI. The results were as follows: $F(1, 87) = .623$, $p = .432$, $\alpha = .05$.

Type of Program and EI (Inferential Statistics)

An independent-samples *t*-test was conducted to compare the levels of emotional intelligence of criminal justice students at an application-based technical college with criminal justice students at a liberal arts non-application-based program. Because the Levene's test was significant, equal variances between the groups is not assumed.

Type of Program and EI
Levene's test is significant; therefore, equal variances not assumed
Dependent Variable: Emotional Intelligence

	Levene's test for Equality of Variance				
	F	Sig	t	df	Sig. (1-tailed)
Equal Variances Assumed	4.445	.038*	2.357	87	.011*
Equal variances not Assumed			2.392	76.654	.010*

*significant at p<.05

31

Dependent Variable: Emotional Intelligence

	N	Mean	SD	SE
Experiential Program	43	134.37	10.599	1.616
Didactic Program	46	127.30	16.778	2.474
Total	89	130.72	14.498	1.537

As predicted, there was a significant difference in the emotional intelligence scores between students in the application-based and non-application-based programs. Criminal justice students at the application-based technical college displayed a higher level of emotional intelligence ($M = 134.37$, $SD = 10.60$, $SE = 1.62$) than did students in the non-application-based liberal arts criminal justice program ($M = 127.30$, $SD = 16.78$, $SE = 2.47$); $t(76.65) = 2.39$, $p \leq .05$, one-tailed. See Appendix for SPSS data output. The effect size was large ($d = .504$) and the power of the statistical test was very good (power $= .762$).

Discussion

The findings indicate that, in this sample, age, gender, and ethnicity were not related to EI. Although Schutte, et al. (1998) has shown that the average score for females (131) is higher than males (125), and the current study also shows that the average score for females (132.2) is higher than males (129.7), the difference is not significant. However, it does demonstrate that the instrument performed as expected. The findings of this study indicate that criminal justice students attending a technical college (i.e., students engaged in experiential learning) had a higher level of emotional intelligence than did criminal justice students attending a liberal arts college (i.e., students engaged in didactic learning).

The curriculums of both schools were compared by the researchers. The curriculum at the technical college has more classes that specifically train students to read body language, to communicate

33

verbally, to perform their jobs objectively (e.g., to control their emotions), to perform their jobs professionally (e.g., to make a good impression to others), and to methodologically investigate problems (e.g., to overcome barriers and contradicting information). Each of these factors were assessed on the Emotional Intelligence Scale and may explain the study's test results. In short, the training that the criminal justice students received at the hands-on technical college may be the factor that distinguished their level of EI from the liberal arts criminal justice students who had little, if any, hands-on training. Thus, a practical implication is that emotional intelligence can be purposively reinforced via training.

Limitations

There were several limitations in the study. First, because the sample was convenient, purposive and non-random, there is a possibility that the participants who chose to participate in the study may be different in meaningful ways from those individuals who chose not to participate. As a result, the findings cannot be generalized to other population groups that do not match the sample's characteristics. Second, Likert-type scales were used and there is the possibility that a) the participants engaged in central tendency bias by simply selecting the middle option instead of the best option, b) the participants engaged in acquiescence bias by simply selecting positive responses over negative responses, and c) due to limited options, the participants were forced to select options that did not accurately represent their perspectives.

Recommendations for Future Research

Due to this being a preliminary study, further studies should be conducted to support whether or not higher levels of EI are developed during the completion of application-based coursework or if there is an inherent difference in individuals who chose a specific type of criminal justice program of study (i.e., there is a concern of causality). In other words, do students learn EI in application-based programs or do students with a higher EI seek application-based programs? Longitudinal studies could also be conducted to assess the relationship between the training of EI in criminal justice coursework and future job performance. If relationships do exist, then perhaps collegiate criminal justice programs that have been strictly academic may wish to consider including some coursework that train students in areas associated with EI. Indeed, enhancing EI may help ensure that graduates are emotionally prepared if they desire to enter the field of law enforcement.

SUMMARY OF STUDY 4

Study #	Focus of Study	Significant Results	Explanation
4	Criminal Justice Students in an experiential program were compared to criminal justice students in a didactic program.	Criminal justice students attending a 2-year technical college with extensive hands-on training displayed a higher level of emotional intelligence than did criminal justice students attending a 4-year liberal arts program with little, if any, hands-on training. Ethnicity, age, and sex were not related to emotional intelligence.	The level of emotional intelligence among criminal justice students varied depending on the type and amount of hands-on training that they received in college. Students in an experiential criminal justice program displayed a higher level of emotional intelligence when compared to criminal justice students in a didactic program.

Summary of Study 4

The evidence has shown that emotional intelligence is directly related to hands-on training. When considering a criminal justice college program, more hands-on training may lead to a higher level of emotional intelligence. Because emotional intelligence may prove beneficial in the field, criminal justice programs may want to consider offerring some application-based courses.

Summary of Study 4 on Emotional Intelligence

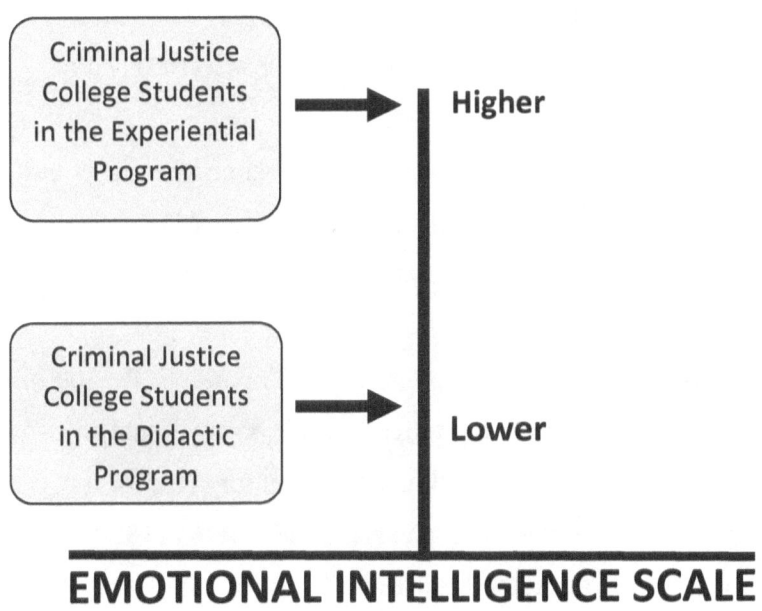

References

Al Ali, O. E., Garner, I., & Magadley, W. (2012). An exploration of the relationship between emotional intelligence and job performance in Police Organizations. *Journal of Police and Criminal Psychology, 27*(1), 1-8. doi: 10.1108/02683940310511890

Bagshaw, M. (2000). Emotional intelligence: Training people to be affective so they can be effective. *Industrial and Commercial Training, 32*(2), 61-65. doi: 10.1108/00197850010320699

Bar-On, R., Brown, J. M., Kirkcaldy, & B. D., Thome', E. P. (2000). Emotional expression and implications for occupational stress; an application of the Emotional Quotient Inventory (EQ-i). *Personality and Individual Differences, 28*, 1107-1118. doi:10.1016/S0191-8869(99)00160-9

Brunetto, Y., Teo, S. T. T., Shacklock, K., & Farr-Wharton, R. (2012). Emotional intelligence, job satisfaction, well-being and engagement: explaining organizational commitment and turnover intentions in policing. *Human Resources Management Journal. 22*(4). doi: 10.1111/j.1748-8583.2012.00198.x

Davis, W. L. & Leslie, P. J. (2014). The effect of application based training on the emotional intelligence of criminal justice students. *Journal of Higher Education Theory and Practice, 14*(2), 115-121.

Deschamps, F., Paganon-Badinier, I., Marchand, A., & Merle, C. (2003). Sources and assessment of occupational stress in the police. *Journal of Occupational Health, 45*, 358-364. doi: 10.1539/joh.45.358

Ellison, K. W. (2004). *Stress and the Police Officer*. Springfield, IL: Charles Thomas.

Greene, H. T., & del Carmen, A. (2002). Female police officers in Texas: perceptions of colleagues and stress. *Policing: An International Journal of Police Strategies and Management, 25*(2), 385-398. doi: 10.1108/13639510210429428

Goleman, D. (1995). *Emotional Intelligence*. New York, NY: Bantam Books.

Goleman, D. (1998). *Working with Emotional Intelligence*. London: Bloomsbury.

He, N., Zhao, J., & Archbold, C. A. (2002). Gender and police stress: The convergent and divergent impact of work environment, work-family conflict, and stress coping mechanisms of female and male officers. *Policing, 25*, 687-708. doi:10.1108/13639510210450631

Latif, D. A. (2004). Using emotional intelligence in the planning and implementation of a management skills course. *Pharmacy Education. 4*(2), 81-89. doi: 10.1080/15602210410001701685

Mayer, J. D., & Salovey, P. (1997). What is emotional intelligence? In Salovey, P. & Sluter, J. (Eds.) *Emotional Development and Emotional Intelligence.* New York, NY: Basic Books.

Norusis, M. J. (2008). *SPSS 16.0 guide to data analysis.* Upper saddle River, NJ: Prentice Hall.

Pogrebin, M. R. & Poole, E. D. (1991). Police and tragic events: The management of emotions. *Journal of Criminal Justice. 19*(4), 395-403. doi:10.1016/0047-2352(91)90036-U

Prazno, P. J. & Prazno, R. (1999). *Stress Management for Law Enforcement: Behind the Shield Combating Trauma.* Longwood, FL: Gould Publications.

Salovey, P. & Mayer, J. D. (1989). Emotional Intelligence. *Imagination, Cognition and Personality, 9*(3), 185-211. doi: 10.2190/DUGG-P24E-52WK-6CDG

Sardo, S. (2004). Learning to display emotional intelligence. *Business Strategy Review, 15*(1), 14-17. doi:10.1111/j.0955-6419.2004.00295.x

Schutte, N. S., Malouff, J. M., Hall, L. E., Haggerty, D. J., Cooper, J. T., Golden, C. J., & Dornheim, L. (1998). Development and validation of a measure of emotional intelligence. *Personality and Individual Differences, 25*, 167-177. doi:10.1016/S0191-8869(98)00001-4

Slaski, M., & Cartwright, S. (2003). Emotional intelligence training and its implications for stress, health and performance. *Stress and Health, 19*(4), 233-239. doi: 10.1002/smi.979

Turner, T. (2006). The need for emotional intelligence in leadership. *FBI Law Enforcement Bulletin. 75*(9), 10.

Weis, W. L., & Arnesen, D. W. (2007). Because EQ can't be told: Doing something about emotional intelligence. *Journal of Organizational Culture, Communications and Conflict, 11*(2), 113.

Zeidner, M., Matthews, G. & Roberts, R. D. (2004). Emotional intelligence in the workplace: A critical review. *Applied Psychology, 53*(3), 371-389. doi: 10.1111/j.1464-0597.2004.00176.x

APPENDIX

Select SPSS Data Results

SPSS Output: Normality of Data, Stem & Leaf

Emotional Intelligence Score Frequency

3.00 Extremes   (=<95)

3.00   10 . 123

2.00   10 . 88

2.00   11 . 44

4.00   11 . 5789

11.00   12 . 00122333344

15.00   12 . 556677788888999

13.00   13 . 0012222233344

12.00   13 . 557778888999

11.00   14 . 00011222334

5.00   14 . 66699

5.00   15 . 00223

3.00   15 . 679

Stem width: 10

Each leaf: 1 case(s)

SPSS Output

Histogram of Emotional Intelligence Scores

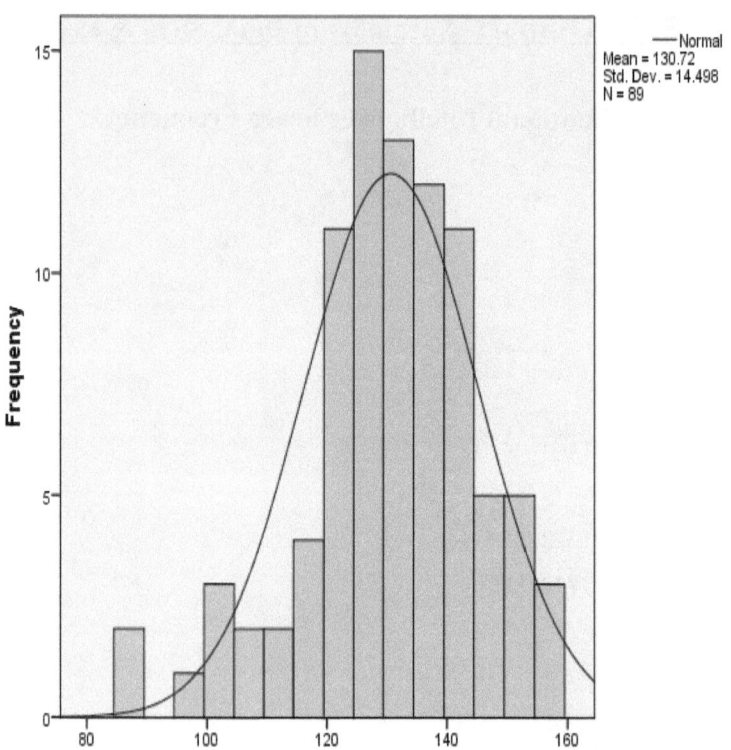

Emotional Intelligence Score

SPSS Output

Boxplot of Emotional Intelligence

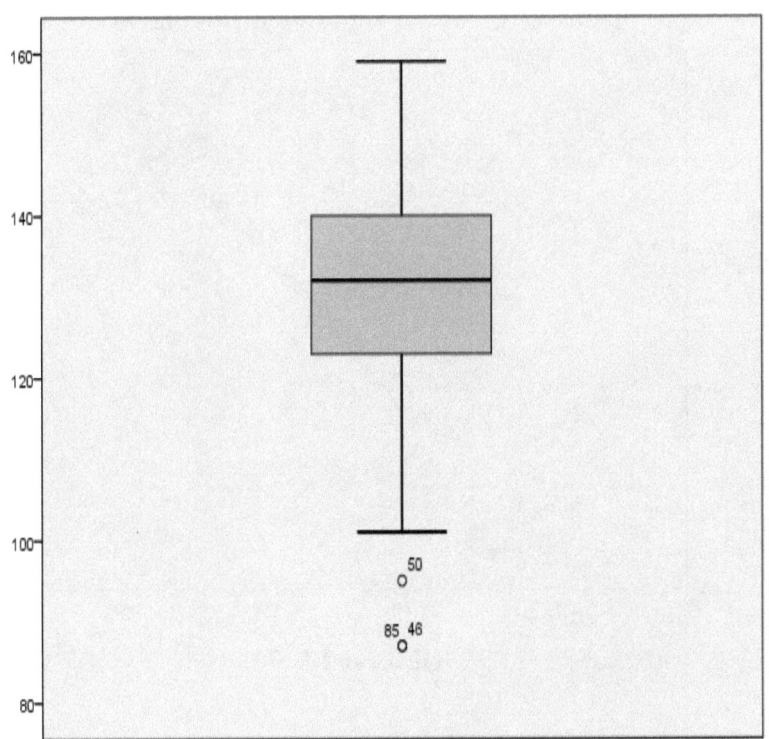

Emotional Intelligence Score

SPSS Output

Q-Q Plot of Emotional Intelligence Scores

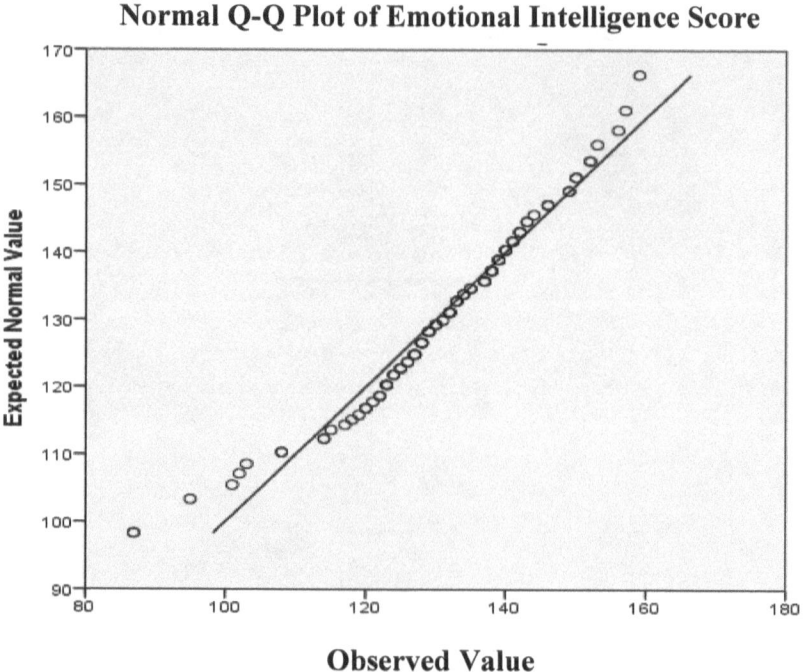

Normal Q-Q Plot of Emotional Intelligence Score

Observed Value

The Q-Q plot (normal probability plot) of emotional intelligence can be used to assess the normality of data. Because the data appear to fall along a straight line, this indicates that the distribution of the dataset is close to normal.

SPSS Output: Age and EI, Regression

Q-Q Plot of Studentized Residuals

Normal Q-Q Plot of Studentized Residual

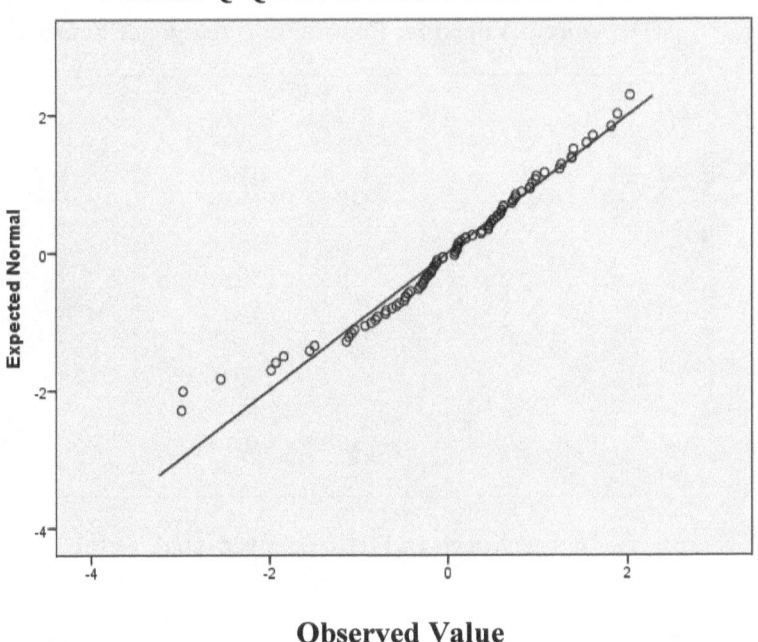

Observed Value

The Q-Q plot (normal probability plot) of Studentized residuals can be used to assess the normality of data. Because the data appear to fall along a straight line, this indicates that the distribution of the dataset is close to normal.

SPSS Output: Age and EI, Regression

Studentized Residuals versus Predicted Values

Scatterplot
Dependent Variable: Emotional Intelligence Score

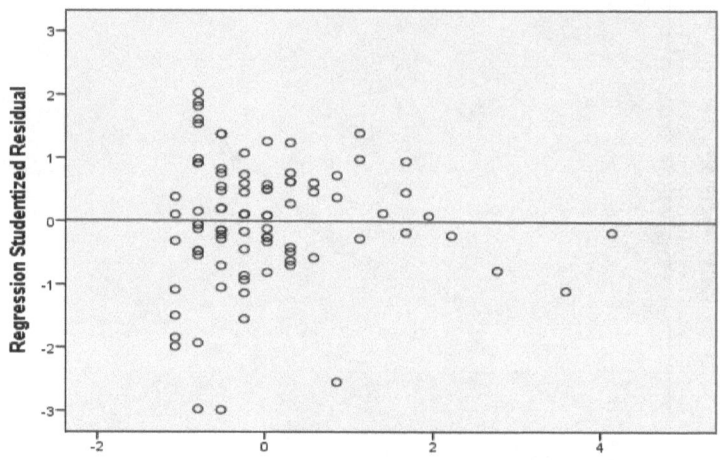

Regression Standardized Predicted Value

The Studentized residual plot indicates that the variance of emotional intelligence is constant across age. In short, because there is no clear pattern in the data values, the variance of emotional intelligence seems to be constant across the independent variable, age.

SPSS Output: Age and EI, Regression

Model Summary[b]

Model	R	R Square	Adjusted R Square	Std. Error of the Estimate
1	.078[a]	.006	-.005	14.536

a. Predictors: (Constant), Age of Student
b. Dependent Variable: Emotional Intelligence Score

ANOVA[a]

Model		Sum of Squares	df	Mean Square	F	Sig.
1	Regression	113.959	1	113.959	.539	.465[b]
	Residual	18382.019	87	211.288		
	Total	18495.978	88			

a. Dependent Variable: Emotional Intelligence Score
b. Predictors: (Constant), Age of Student

Coefficients[a]

Model		Unstandardized Coefficients		Standardized Coefficients	t	Sig.
		B	Std. Error	Beta		
1	(Constant)	123.891	9.425		13.146	.000
	Age of Student	.312	.425	.078	.734	.465

a. Dependent Variable: Emotional Intelligence Score

Summary of Age and EI

$F(1,87) = .539$, p $= .465$ (not significant)

EI $= 123.891 + .312$ (age), R2 $= .006$

There is no significant relationship between age and EI. Age is a poor predictor of EI.

SPSS Output: Difference between Ethnicity and EI, ANOVA

ANOVA

Emotional Intelligence Score

	Sum of Squares	df	Mean Square	F	Sig.
Between Groups	59.845	3	19.948	.092	.964
Within Groups	18436.132	85	216.896		
Total	18495.978	88			

Summary of Ethnicity and EI

$F(3,85) = .092$, p = .964   (not significant at $\alpha = .05$)

There are no significant differences between ethnicity groups and EI.

SPSS Output: Difference between Gender and EI, ANOVA

Dependent Variable: Emotional Intelligence

	N	Mean	SD	SE
Females	35	132.23	14.955	2.528
Males	54	129.74	14.246	1.939
Total	89	130.72	14.498	1.537

ANOVA

Emotional Intelligence Score

	Sum of Squares	df	Mean Square	F	Sig.
Between Groups	131.436	1	131.436	.623	.432
Within Groups	18364.542	87	211.087		
Total	18495.978	88			

Summary of Gender and EI

$F(1,87) = .623$, p = .432   (not significant at $\alpha = .05$)

There is no significant difference between gender and EI.

SPSS Output: Type of Program and EI,

Independent-samples t-Test

Group Statistics

	College Degree Program	N	Mean	Std. Deviation	Std. Error Mean
Emotional Intelligence Score	1 (Experiential Program)	43	134.37	10.599	1.616
	2 (Didactic Program)	46	127.30	16.778	2.474

Independent Samples Test

		Levene's Test for Equality of Variances		t-test for Equality of Means
		F	Sig.	t
Emotional Intelligence Score	Equal variances assumed	4.445	.038	2.357
	Equal variances not assumed			2.392

SPSS Output: Type of Program and EI,

Independent-samples t-Test

Independent Samples Test

		t-test for Equality of Means		
		df	Sig. (2-tailed)	Mean Difference
Emotional Intelligence Score	Equal variances assumed	87	.021	7.068
	Equal variances not assumed	76.654	.019	7.068

Summary of Criminal Justice Programs

$M_1 = 134.37$, $SD_1 = 10.60$, $SE_1 = 1.62$

$M_2 = 127.30$, $SD_2 = 16.78$, $SE_2 = 2.47$

$t(76.65) = 2.39$, $p \leq .05$, one-tailed

There is a significant difference between the criminal justice programs and EI.

www.ingramcontent.com/pod-product-compliance
Lightning Source LLC
Chambersburg PA
CBHW030529290526
45786CB00004B/1660